From Here to There
with
Cuisenaire Rods

by
Patricia S. Davidson
Robert E. Willcutt

Cuisenaire Company of America, Inc.
10 Bank Street. P.O. Box 5026
White Plains, NY 10602-5026

A Special Note To Teachers

The goal of this workbook is for students to use the rods to develop the concepts of area, perimeter, surface area and volume. Interrelationships between these concepts are also explored through patterns and puzzles which can help to enhance students' problem solving abilities, especially their spatial abilities. Students should be encouraged to use the rods in solving all problems so that the concepts will have a concrete foundation. Centimeter graph paper should be made available for students to show exploratory work and alternate answers. Students may wish to use the metric aspects of the rods by recording units in centimeters for perimeter, square centimeters for area and surface area, and cubic centimeters for volume. This workbook is intended for students in Grades 4-8.

Copyright © 1981 by
Cuisenaire Company of America, Inc
10 Bank Street, PO Box 5026, White Plains, NY 10602-5026

ISBN 0-914040-88-X

Printed in U.S.A.

3 4 5 6 7 8 9 10-BK-98 97 96

Table of Contents

Stamping Footprints with Rods

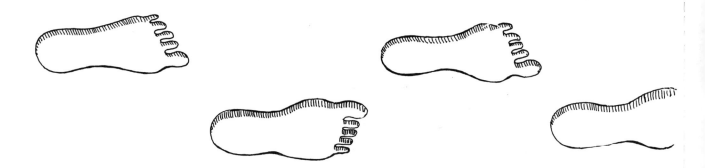

Take a purple rod and pretend to stamp its footprint by placing it on graph paper.

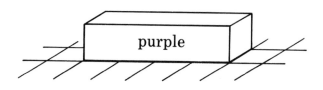

Trace with your pencil the outline of the footprint for the purple rod on the graph paper below.

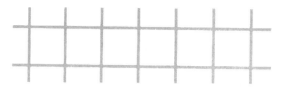

Your tracing should look like this:

Count the number of squares. There are 4.

You have just found the AREA enclosed by the outline of the purple rod. The area is 4 square units.

From Here to There With Cuisenaire Rods   © 1981 Cuisenaire Company of America. Inc.

Stamping Footprints with Rods

1) Pretend to stamp a footprint of a yellow rod by placing it on the graph paper below. Trace its outline with your pencil.

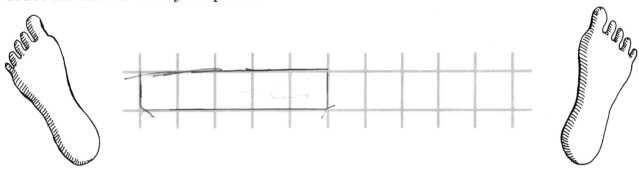

Count the number of squares enclosed by the outline. The area enclosed by the outline of the yellow rod = ___5___ square units.

Pretend to stamp a footprint for each of the following rods on the graph paper below. Trace to find the area enclosed by the outline of each rod.

2) black

Area = ___7___ square units

3) brown

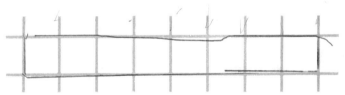

Area = ___9___ square units

4) orange

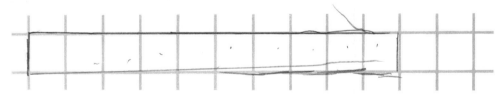

Area = ___10___ square units

5) Explore the footprints for the other rod colors.

Finding Area of Rod Designs

Use the designated number of rods as footprints to cover each rod design. Record the color names to show how you placed the rods on each design. Find the area of each rod design. (Let ☐ = 1 square unit.)

1) Use two rods.

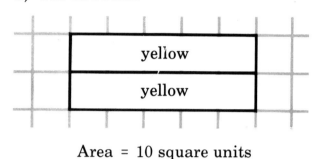

Area = 10 square units

2) Use eight rods.

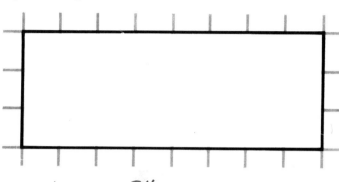

Area = ___24___ square units

3) Use three rods.

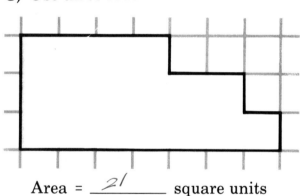

Area = ___21___ square units

4) Use four rods.

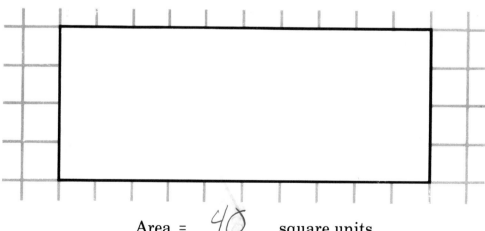

Area = ___40___ square units

From Here to There with Cuisenaire Rods

Finding Area of Rod Designs

Use the designated number of rods as footprints to cover each rod design. Record the color names to show how you placed the rods on each design. Find the area of each rod design. (Let ☐ = 1 square unit.)

1) Use six rods.

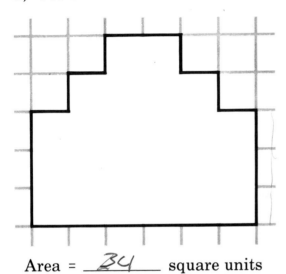

Area = _____34_____ square units

2) Use six rods.

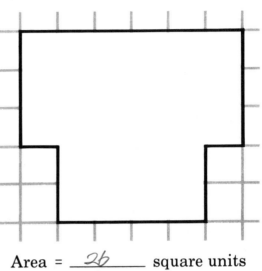

Area = _____26_____ square units

3) Use eight rods

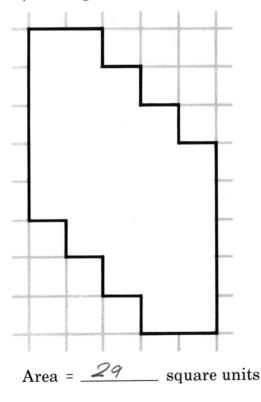

Area = _____29_____ square units

4) Use nine rods

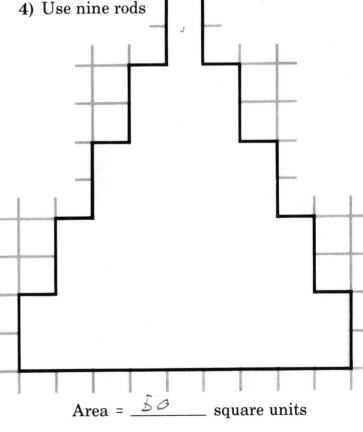

Area = _____50_____ square units

Finding Area in Different Ways

This design can be covered with rods in different ways. Place rods as shown below and compute the area. Check that you get the same value for the area of the design. (Let ☐ = 1 square unit.)

1)

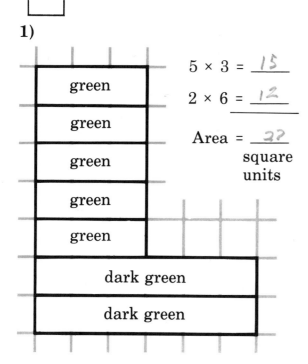

5 × 3 = _15_

2 × 6 = _12_

Area = _27_ square units

2)

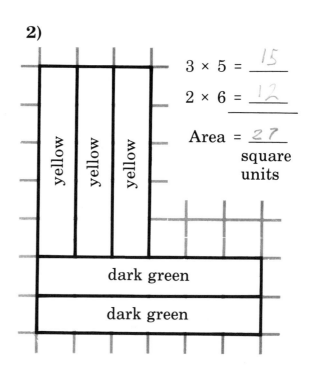

3 × 5 = _15_

2 × 6 = _12_

Area = _27_ square units

3)

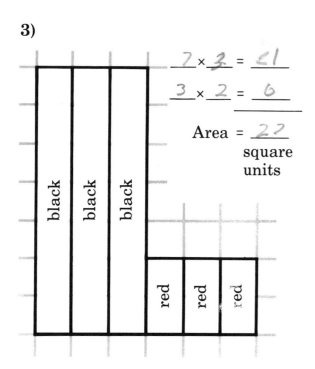

_7_ × _3_ = _21_

_3_ × _2_ = _6_

Area = _27_ square units

4) Cover this same design with rods in your own way. Compute the area.

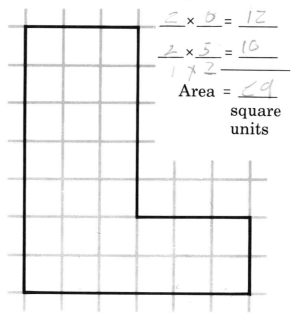

_2_ × _6_ = _12_

_2_ × _5_ = _10_

_1_ × _2_ _____

Area = _27_ square units

From Here to There With Cuisenaire Rods © 1981 Cuisenaire Company of America, Inc.

Finding Area in Different Ways

This design can be covered with rods in different ways. Place rods as shown below and compute the area. Check that you get the same value for the area of the design.
(Let ☐ = 1 square unit.)

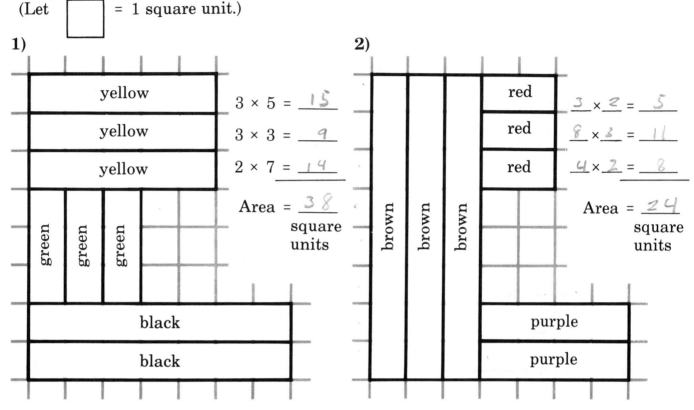

1)

yellow

3 × 5 = _15_

yellow

3 × 3 = _9_

yellow

2 × 7 = _14_

green green green

Area = _38_ square units

black

black

2)

brown brown brown

red

3 × 2 = _5_

red

8 × 3 = _11_

red

4 × 2 = _8_

Area = _24_ square units

purple

purple

Now cover the design with rods in your own ways. Record the color names to show how you placed the rods on each design. Then compute the area.

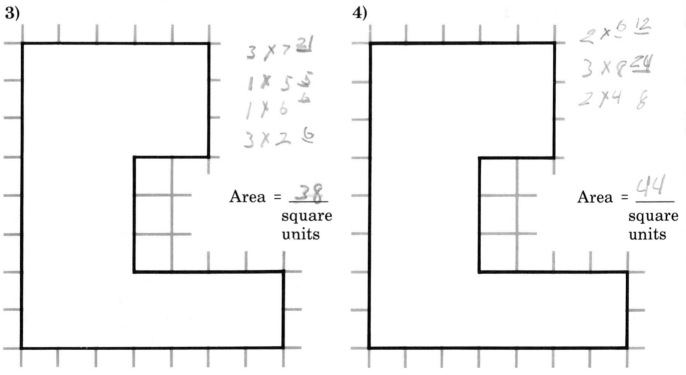

3)

3 × 7 = 21
1 × 5 = 5
1 × 6 = 6
3 × 2 = 6

Area = _38_ square units

4)

2 × 6 = 12
3 × 8 = 24
2 × 4 = 8

Area = _44_ square units

Finding Area in Different Ways

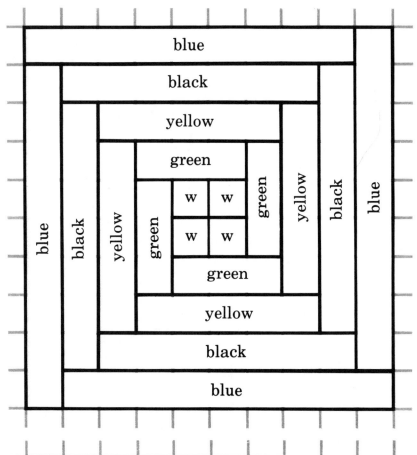

1) Place rods as shown to form the square. Compute the area.
(Let ⬜ = 1 square unit.)

$4 \times 9 = $ _____

$4 \times 7 = $ _____

$4 \times$ ___ $= $ _____

___ $\times$ ___ $= $ _____

___ $\times$ ___ $= $ _____

_____

Area = _____

square units

2) Now cover the square with rods in your own way. Show your computation for the area.

$\underline{3} \times \underline{7} = \underline{21}$

$\underline{3} \times \underline{8} = \underline{24}$

$\underline{5} \times \underline{3} = \underline{15}$

$\underline{3} \times \underline{2} = \underline{6}$

$\underline{2} \times \underline{6} = \underline{12}$

_____

Area = $\underline{28}$

square units

Check with your classmates that all the different ways result in the same value for the area.

From Here to There with Cuisenaire Rods

Finding Area in Different Ways

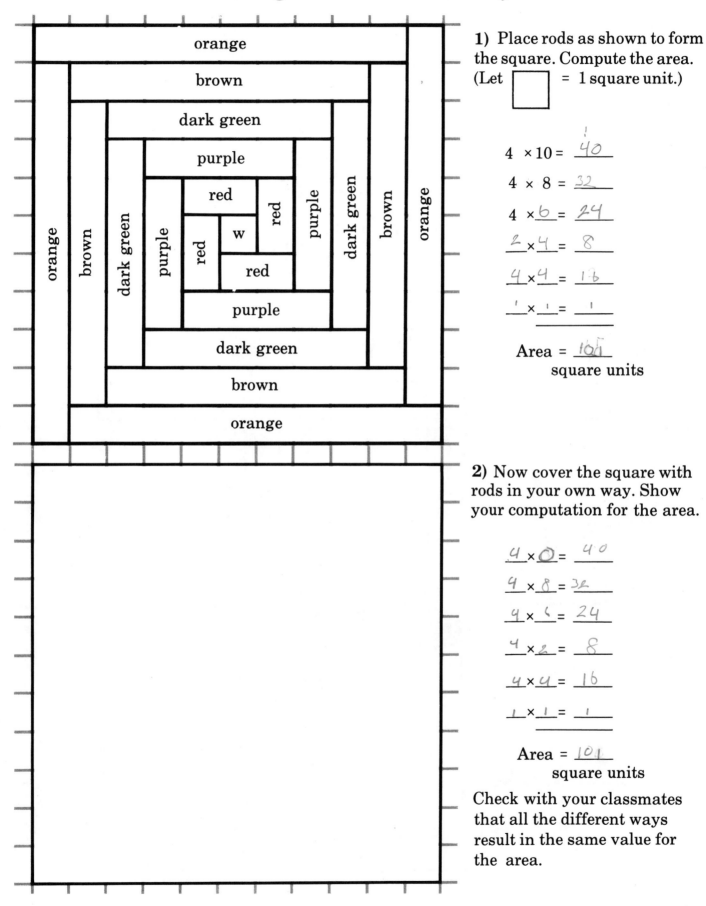

1) Place rods as shown to form the square. Compute the area.
(Let ☐ = 1 square unit.)

4 × 10 = 40

4 × 8 = 32

4 × 6 = 24

2 × 4 = 8

4 × 4 = 16

1 × 1 = 1

Area = 101
square units

2) Now cover the square with rods in your own way. Show your computation for the area.

4 × 0 = 4·0

4 × 8 = 32

4 × 6 = 24

4 × 2 = 8

4 × 4 = 16

1 × 1 = 1

Area = 101
square units

Check with your classmates that all the different ways result in the same value for the area.

Finding Area of Rod Pictures

Cover the shaded regions with rods. Find the area.   (Let $\boxed{103}$ = 1 square unit.)

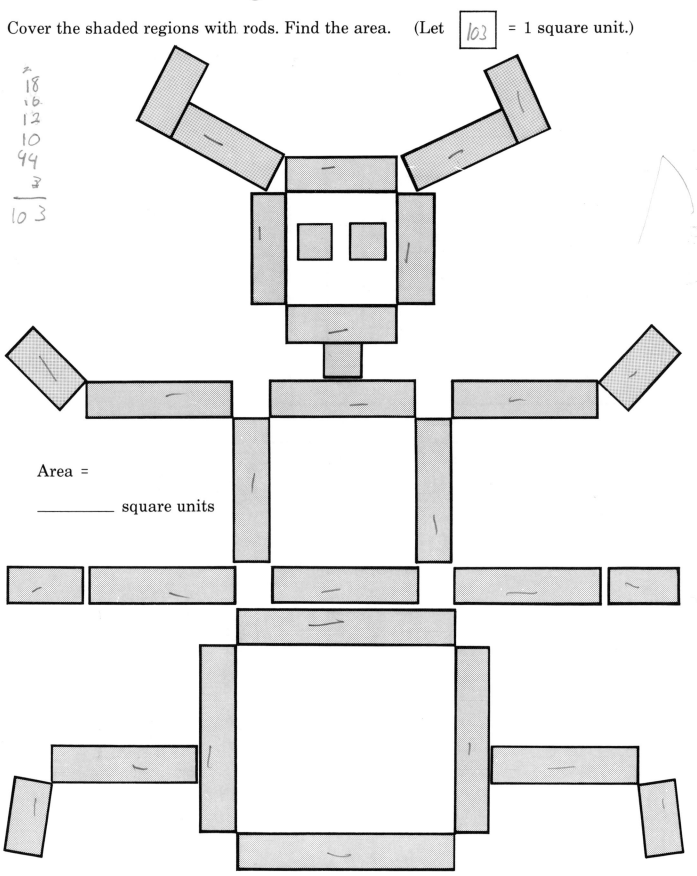

2
18
16
12
10
44
3
———
103

Area =

_____ square units

From Here to There With Cuisenaire Rods   © 1981 Cuisenaire Company of America, Inc.

Finding Area of Rod Pictures

Cover these shaded regions with rods. Find the area of each. Then make a rod picture of your own and have a classmate compute the area. (Let ☐ = 1 square unit.)

1)   **2)**

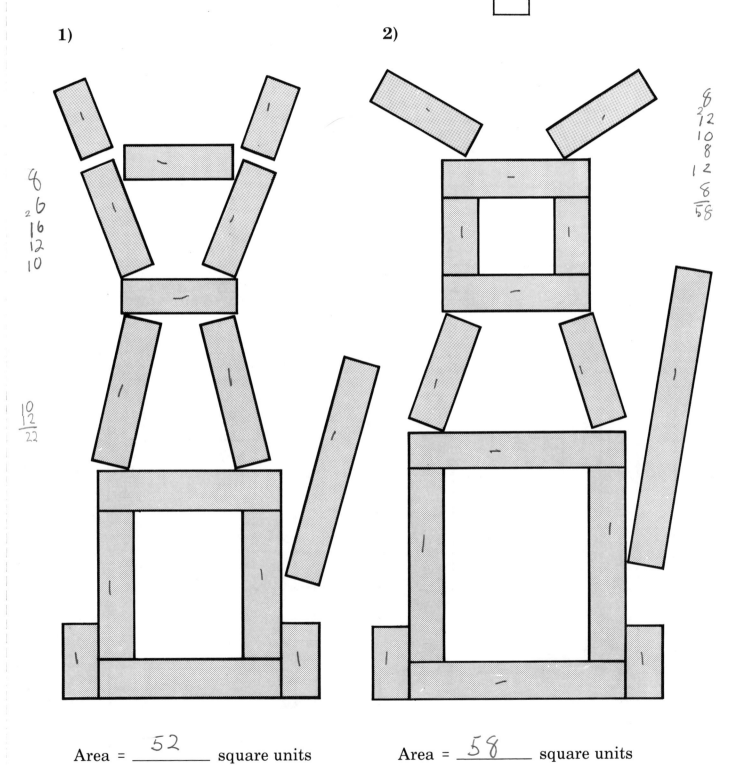

Area = _____52_____ square units   Area = _____58_____ square units

Finding Area of Rod Designs

Cover each shape using the number of rods indicated. Then find the area of each rod design. (Let ⬜ = 1 square unit.)

1) Use seven rods.
    2) Use ten rods.

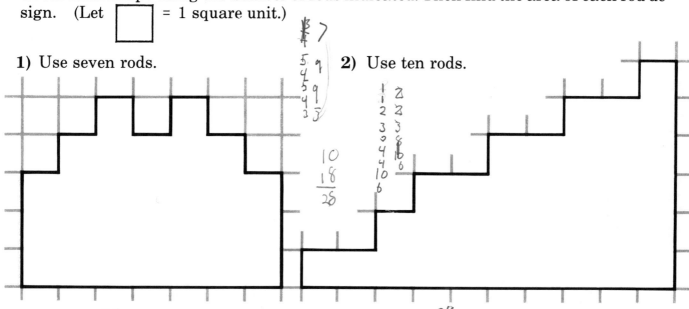

Area = __28__ square units
    Area = __34__ square units

3) Use nine rods.

4) Use seven rods.

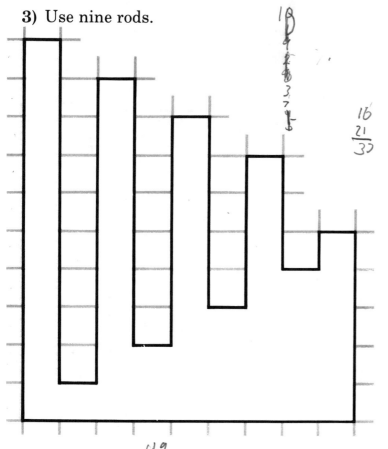

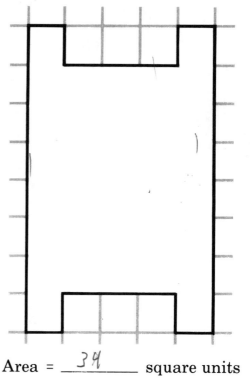

Area = __34__ square units

Area = __49__ square units

What is the minimum number of rods needed for each design?

1) _____ 2) _____ 3) _____ 4) _____

     From Here to There With Cuisenaire Rods

Finding Area of Rod Designs

Cover each shape as indicated. Then find the area of each rod design. (Let ▢ = 1 square unit.)

1) Use fewer than ten rods.

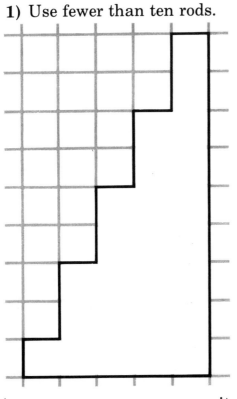

Area = _____ square units

2) Use fewer than eight rods.

Area =

_____

square units

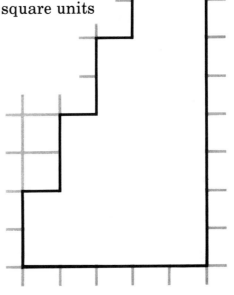

3) Use fewer than twelve rods.

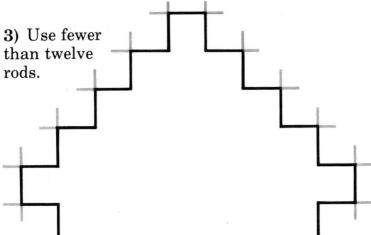

Area =

_____

square units

4) Use fewer than nine rods.

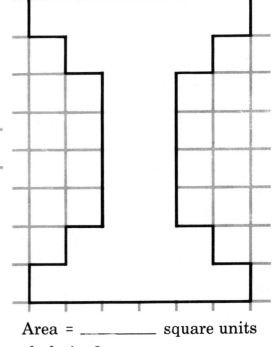

Area = _____ square units

What is the minimum number of rods needed for each design?

1) _____ 2) _____ 3) _____ 4) _____

Finding Area of Rod Designs

Cover each shape as indicated. Then find the area. (Let 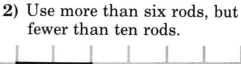 = 1 square unit.)

1) Use more than seven rods, but fewer than eleven rods.

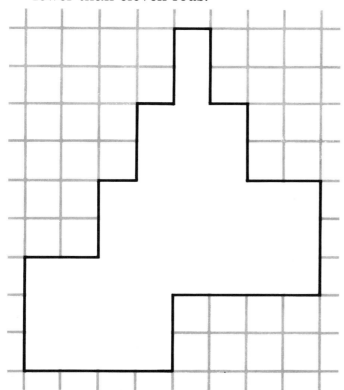

Area = _____ square units

2) Use more than six rods, but fewer than ten rods.

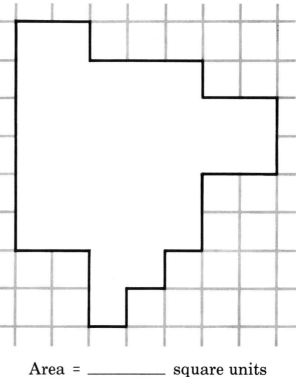

Area = _____ square units

3) Use more than five rods, but fewer than nine rods.

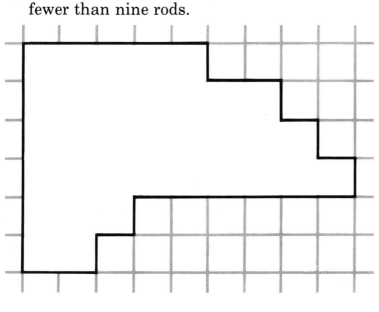

Area = _____ square units

4) Use more than six rods, but fewer than twelve rods.

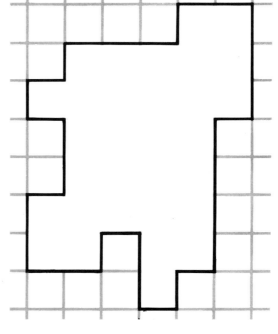

Area = _____ square units

From Here to There With Cuisenaire Rods

Finding Area of Rod Designs

Cover each shape as indicated. Then find the area. (Let $\square$ = 1 square unit.)

1) Use more than six rods, but fewer than twelve rods.

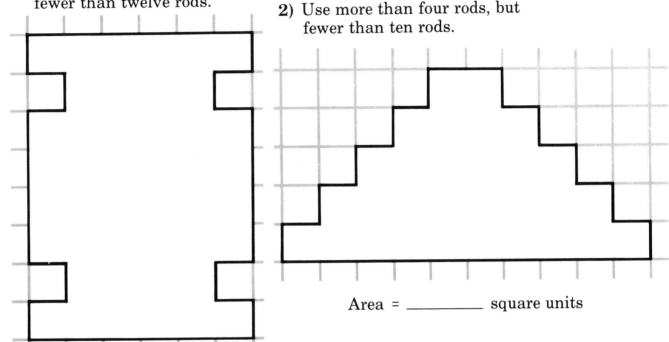

Area = _____ square units

2) Use more than four rods, but fewer than ten rods.

Area = _____ square units

3) Use more than eight rods, but fewer than thirteen rods.

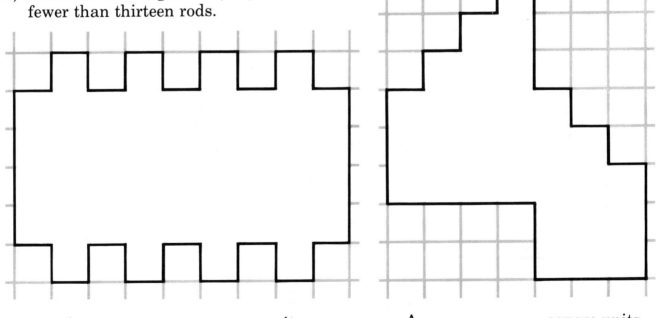

Area = _____ square units

4) Use more than five rods, but fewer than ten rods.

Area = _____ square units

Solving Area Puzzles

Cover each shape with rods to find the area. (Let ⬚ = 1 square unit.)

1)

Find the area of this figure.

Area = _____ square units
What is the fewest number of
rods needed to build this figure? _____
What is the greatest number
of rods that you could use? _____

2)

Area = _____ square units
Fewest number
of rods needed? _____
Greatest number
of rods that you could use? _____

3)

Area = _____ square units
Fewest number of rods needed? _____
Greatest number of rods that you could use? _____

From Here to There With Cuisenaire Rods   © 1981 Cuisenaire Company of America, Inc.

Solving Area Puzzles

(Let ☐ = 1 square unit.)

1) Here is a ten-sided figure with an area of 28 square units. What is the fewest number of rods needed to build this figure? _____

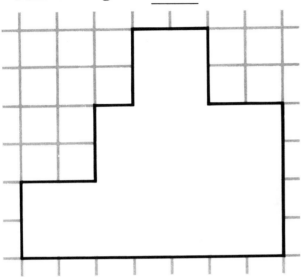

2) Make a six-sided figure with an area of 24 square units. Use no rods shorter than a light green rod.

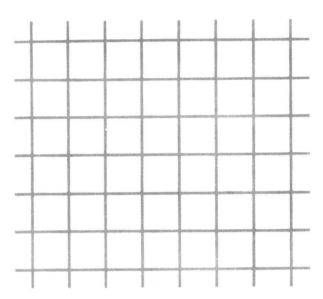

3) Make an eight-sided figure with an area of 37 square units. Use no rod shorter than a purple rod.

4) Make a ten-sided figure with an area of 33 square units. Use no rod shorter than a purple rod.

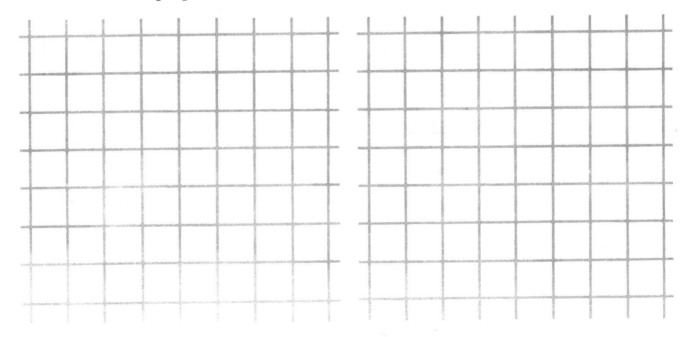

Finding the Distance Around

Take a dark green rod and place it on the graph paper, like this:

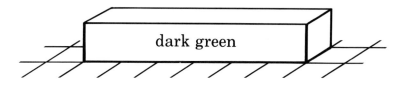

Trace with your pencil the outline of the dark green rod.

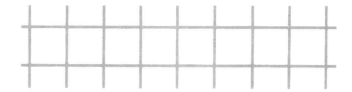

Your tracing should look like this:

Count the number of units of length in the outline of the dark green rod. There are 14.

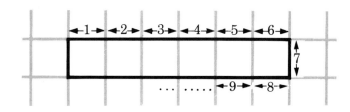

You have just found the PERIMETER of the outline of the dark green rod as 14 units of length.

From Here to There With Cuisenaire Rods

Finding the Distance Around

1)

yellow

Place a yellow rod on this strip of graph paper and trace its outline with your pencil.

Count the number of units of length in the outline to find the perimeter.

Perimeter = _____ units

2)

purple

Trace to find the perimeter of the outline of a purple rod.

Perimeter = _____ units

3)

black

Trace to find the perimeter of the outline of a black rod.

Perimeter = _____ units

4)

brown

Trace to find the perimeter of the outline of a brown rod.

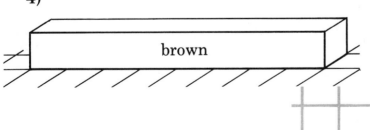

Perimeter = _____ units

Finding Perimeter of Rod Designs

1) Place three purple rods on the graph paper at the right below. Trace around the outline to find the perimeter of the rod design, as shown.

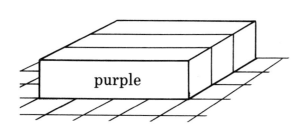

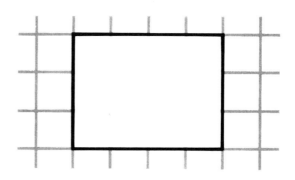

Perimeter = _____ units

2) Place four yellow rods on the graph paper at the right below. Trace around the outline to find the perimeter of the rod design.

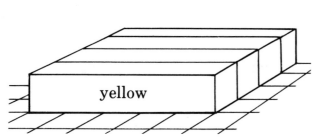

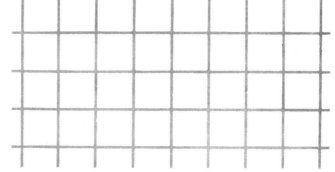

Perimeter = _____ units

3) Place four dark green rods on the graph paper at the right below. Trace around the outline to find the perimeter of the rod design.

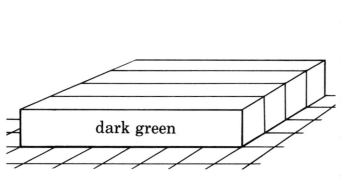

Perimeter = _____ units

From Here to There With Cuisenaire Rods   © 1981 Cuisenaire Company of America, Inc.

Finding Perimeter of Rod Designs

Place rods to make each design below. Record the color names to show how you place the rods on each design. Find the perimeter of each rod design.

1)

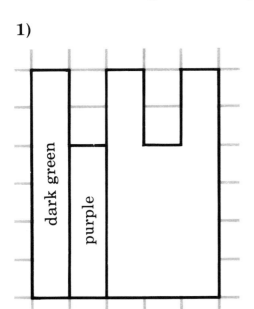

Perimeter = _____ units

2)

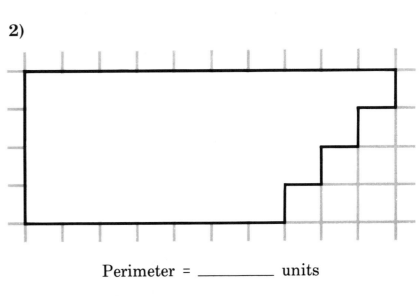

Perimeter = _____ units

3)

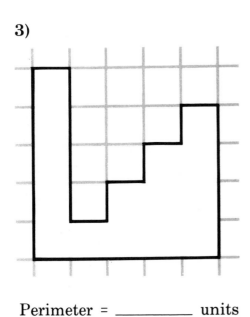

Perimeter = _____ units

4)

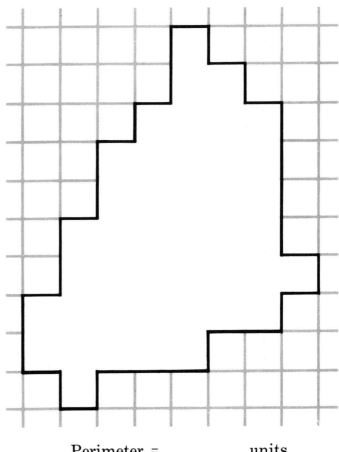

Perimeter = _____ units

Finding Different Perimeters

All of these rod designs can be made with the same three rod colors: <u>green</u>, <u>purple</u>, and <u>yellow</u>. Record how you place the rods on the designs. Find the perimeter of each rod design.

1)

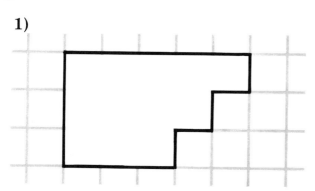

Perimeter = _____ units

2)

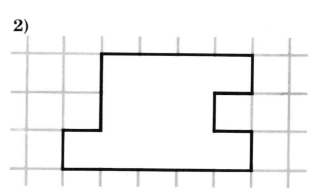

Perimeter = _____ units

3)

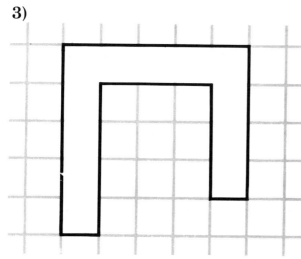

Perimeter = _____ units

4)

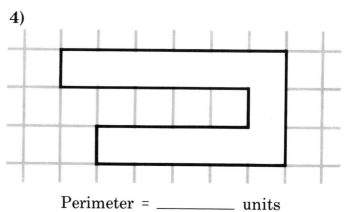

Perimeter = _____ units

5)

Perimeter = _____ units

6)

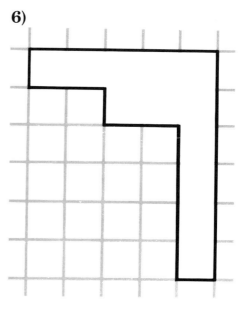

Perimeter = _____ units

From Here to There With Cuisenaire Rods © 1981 Cuisenaire Company of America, Inc.

Finding Different Perimeters

Take a <u>red</u>, <u>yellow</u>, and <u>dark green</u> rod. Make each of these designs and find its perimeter.

1)

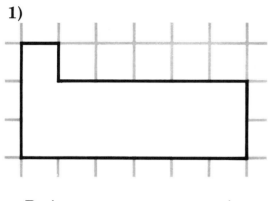

Perimeter = _____ units

2)

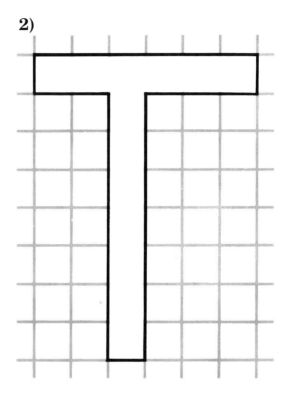

Perimeter = _____ units

Now trace around three more designs on the graph paper below, each using a <u>red</u>, <u>yellow</u>, and <u>dark green</u> rod. Find the perimeters.

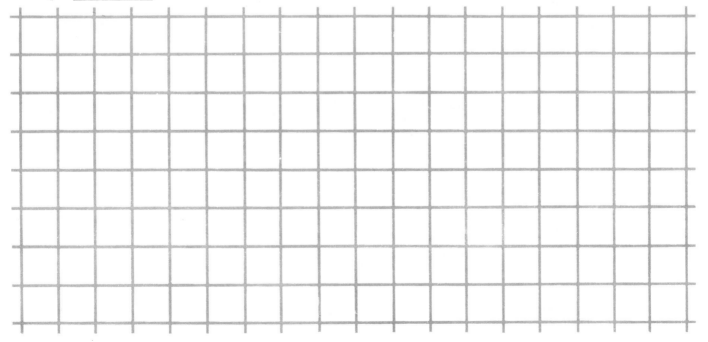

3) Perimeter = _____ units   **4)** Perimeter = _____ units   **5)** Perimeter = _____ units

Finding Different Perimeters

Use these four rods to make a rod design with the given perimeter: <u>red</u>, <u>green</u>, <u>green</u>, <u>purple</u>.

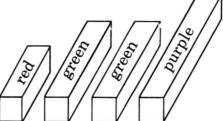

Here is one way to create a perimeter of 22 units.

1) Show a different design with perimeter 22.

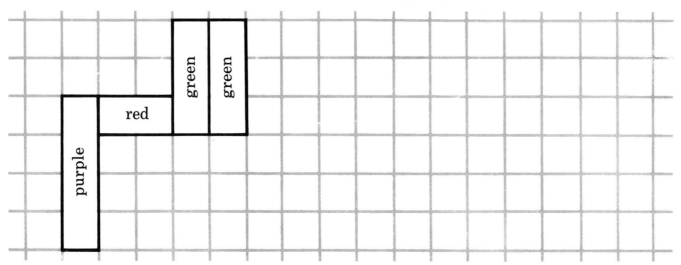

Now find one possible design for each of the following perimeters, using <u>red</u>, <u>green</u>, <u>green</u>, <u>purple</u>. Trace around your designs.

2) 14 units   **3)** 16 units   **4)** 18 units   **5)** 20 units   **6)** 26 units

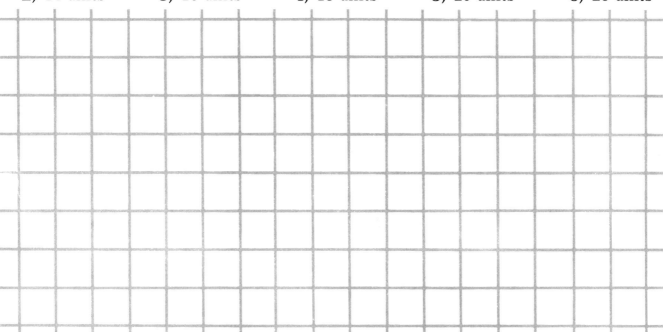

     From Here to There With Cuisenaire Rods

Solving Perimeter Puzzles

Solve each puzzle. Trace around your rod designs and record how the given rods were used to create the given perimeter.

1) Use these three rods to make a design

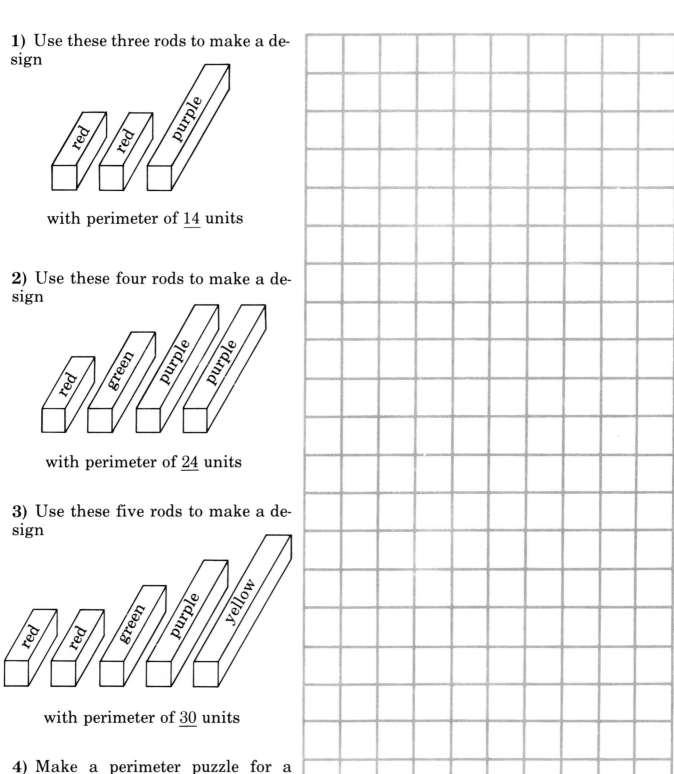

with perimeter of <u>14</u> units

2) Use these four rods to make a design

with perimeter of <u>24</u> units

3) Use these five rods to make a design

with perimeter of <u>30</u> units

4) Make a perimeter puzzle for a classmate to solve.

Making Rectangles with Constant Area

Take 36 white rods and make as many different rectangles as possible, each with an area of 36 square units. (Let ☐ = 1 square unit.)

Example: This rectangle has dimensions 4 × 9.

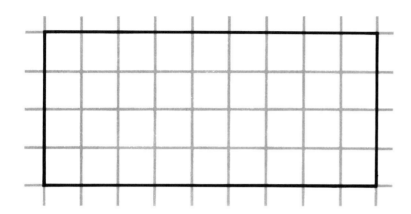

The area is 36 square units.
The perimeter is 26 units.

Fill in the table for each of your rectangles.

Width	Length	Area (square units)	Perimeter (units)
4	9	36	26
——	——	36	——
——	——	36	——
——	——	36	——
——	——	36	——
——	——	36	——
——	——	36	——
——	——	36	——
——	——	36	——

Although there is the same or "constant area" for each rectangle, the perimeters are different.

What are the dimensions of the rectangle with the minimum perimeter of 24 units?_____

From Here to There with Cuisenaire Rods

Making Rectangles with Constant Areas

Fill in the tables for each of the following rectangles. (Let $\boxed{}$ = 1 square unit.)

1) Constant Area: 16 square units

Width	Length	Area (square units)	Perimeter (units)
1	___	16	___
2	___	16	___
4	___	16	___
8	___	16	___
16	___	16	___

Dimensions of the rectangle with minimum perimeter: _____

2) Constant Area: 25 square units

Width	Length	Area (square units)	Perimeter (units)
1	___	25	___
5	___	25	___
25	___	25	___

Dimensions of the rectangle with minimum perimeter: _____

3) Constant Area: 64 square units

Width	Length	Area (square units)	Perimeter (units)
1	___	64	___
2	___	64	___
4	___	64	___
8	___	64	___
16	___	64	___
32	___	64	___
64	___	64	___

Dimensions of the rectangle with minimum perimeter: _____

4) Constant Area: 100 square units

Width	Length	Area (square units)	Perimeter (units)
1	___	100	___
2	___	100	___
4	___	100	___
5	___	100	___
10	___	100	___
20	___	100	___
25	___	100	___
50	___	100	___
100	___	100	___

Dimensions of the rectangle with minimum perimeter: _____

Making Rectangles with Constant Perimeter

These rectangles have a perimeter of 24 units.

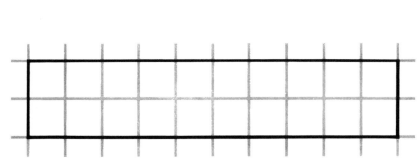

Dimensions: 2 × 10

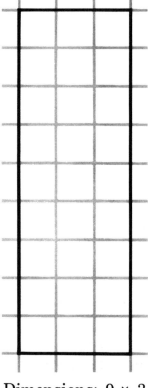

Dimensions: 9 × 3

Fill in the table for all the possible rectangles with a perimeter of 24 units.

Width	Length	Perimeter (units)	Area (square units)
1	____	24	____
2	10	24	20
3	____	24	____
4	____	24	____
5	____	24	____
6	____	24	____
7	____	24	____
8	____	24	____
9	____	24	____
10	____	24	____
11	____	24	____

Look for patterns in the table.

What are the dimensions of the rectangle with the maximum area? _____

From Here to There with Cuisenaire Rods   © 1981 Cuisenaire Company of America, Inc.

Making Rectangles with Constant Perimeters

Fill in the tables for each of the following rectangles.

1) Constant Perimeter: 12 units

Width	Length	Perimeter (units)	Area (square units)
1	___	12	___
2	___	12	___
3	___	12	___
4	___	12	___
5	___	12	___

Dimensions of the rectangle with maximum area: _____

2) Constant Perimeter: 20 units

Width	Length	Perimeter (units)	Area (square units)
1	___	20	___
2	___	20	___
3	___	20	___
4	___	20	___
5	___	20	___
6	___	20	___
7	___	20	___
8	___	20	___
9	___	20	___

Dimensions of the rectangle with maximum area: _____

3) Constant Perimeter: 28 units

Width	Length	Perimeter (units)	Area (square units)
1	___	28	___
2	___	28	___
3	___	28	___
4	___	28	___
5	___	28	___
6	___	28	___
7	___	28	___
8	___	28	___
9	___	28	___
10	___	28	___
11	___	28	___
12	___	28	___
13	___	28	___

Dimensions of the rectangle with maximum area: _____

4) Constant Perimeter: 32 units

Width	Length	Perimeter (units)	Area (square units)
1	___	32	___
2	___	32	___
3	___	32	___
4	___	32	___
5	___	32	___
6	___	32	___
7	___	32	___
8	___	32	___
9	___	32	___
10	___	32	___
11	___	32	___
12	___	32	___
13	___	32	___
14	___	32	___
15	___	32	___

Dimensions of the rectangle with maximum area: _____

Solving Area and Perimeter Problems

(Let ☐ = 1 square unit.)

1) Use these seven rods to make a figure with an area of 26 square units and a perimeter of 26 units.

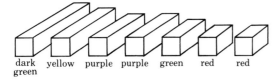

dark green · yellow · purple · purple · green · red · red

2) Use the same seven rods to create an 8 sided figure with an area of 26 square units and a perimeter of 34 units.

3) Still using the same seven rods, create a 12 sided figure with an area of 26 square units and a perimeter of 40 units.

4) Use these eight rods to make a design with 8 sides, a perimeter of 32 units and an area of 34 square units.

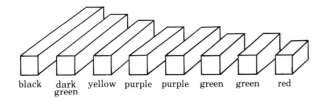

black · dark green · yellow · purple · purple · green · green · red

5) Use the same eight rods to create a figure with 12 sides, a perimeter of 40 units and an area of 34 square units.

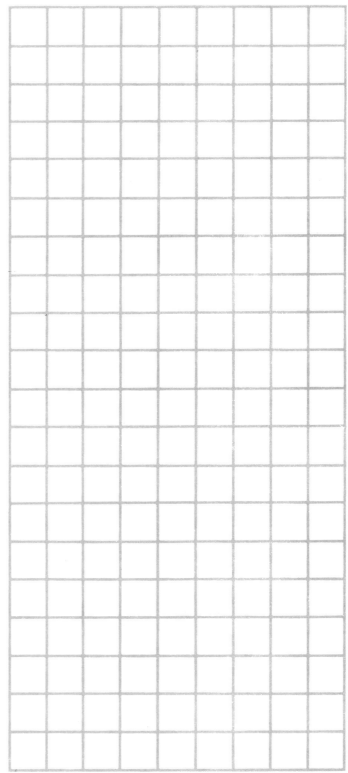

From Here to There with Cuisenaire Rods

Solving Area and Perimeter Problems

(Let ⬜ = 1 square unit.)

1) Create a figure with an area of 25 square units and a perimeter of 28 units. Use no rods shorter than a purple rod or larger than a dark green rod.

2) Make a figure which has 8 sides, an area of 28 square units, and a perimeter of 24 units. Use no rods shorter than a green rod or longer than a yellow rod.

3) For a final challenge, use exactly 8 rods, (no rod shorter than a red rod or longer than a dark green rod) to create an 8 sided figure with an area of 35 square units and a perimeter of 42 units.

Painting Rod Lengths

Take a yellow rod and a white rod. Pretend that the white rod is a rubber stamp and that you are going to paint one surface of the yellow rod length. The fewest number of times that you have to stamp this surface is 5.

Now pretend that you want to paint the entire surface of a yellow rod.

The fewest number of times that you have to stamp the entire surface is 22 (four rod lengths plus the two ends). You have just found the SURFACE AREA of a yellow rod as 22 square units.

Now do the same for a dark green rod. How many times do you need to stamp one surface of a dark green length? _____

How many times do you need to stamp the entire surface of a dark green rod? _____
What is the surface area of a dark green rod? _____

From Here to There with Cuisenaire Rods   © 1981 Cuisenaire Company of America, Inc.

Painting Rod Surfaces

Pretend that the white rod is a rubber stamp and that you are going to paint the entire surface of each rod in the staircase. Fill in the table for the surface areas, S.

Color	Length L	Surface area S
white	1	____
red	2	____
green	3	____
purple	4	____
yellow	5	22
dark green	6	26
black	7	____
brown	8	____
blue	9	____
orange	10	____

Look for patterns in your table. Explain why the surface area values increase by 4.

The formula S = (4 × L) + 2 describes the surface area values. The surface area is made up of 4 lengths plus the 2 ends. Verify that this formula works for all the rod lengths.

Painting Two Rods Glued Together

Pretend that the white rod is a rubber stamp and that you are going to paint the entire surface of two rods glued together in the following way:

Fill in the table for the surface area of the two rods glued together, T.

Color	Length L	S	T
white	1	6	____
red	2	10	____
green	3	14	____
purple	4	18	____
yellow	5	22	34 { How many lengths? _____ How many ends? _____
dark green	6	26	____
black	7	30	____
brown	8	34	____
blue	9	38	____
orange	10	42	____

Look for patterns in your table. Explain why the surface area values for the two glued rods increase by 6.

Explain the formula T = (6 × L) + 4.

Explain the formula T = (2 × S) – (2 × L).

Show that both of these formulas check the values in the table.

From Here to There with Cuisenaire Rods   © 1981 Cuisenaire Company of America, Inc.

Painting Two Rods Glued Together

Pretend that the white rod is a rubber stamp and that you are going to paint the entire surface area of two rods glued end-to-end.

Fill in the table for the surface area of the two rods glued end-to-end, E.

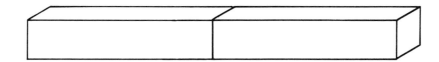

Color	Length L	S	E
white	1	6	_____
red	2	10	_____
green	3	14	_____
purple	4	18	_____
yellow	5	22	42 {How many lengths? _____ How many ends? _____
dark green	6	26	_____
black	7	30	_____
brown	8	34	_____
blue	9	38	_____
orange	10	42	_____

Look for patterns in your table.

Write the formula: E = (____ × L) + ____. Explain.

Write the formula: E = (____ × S) − ____. Explain.

Show that both of these formulas check the values in this table.

Painting Three Rods Glued Together

Pretend that the white rod is a rubber stamp and that you are going to paint the entire surface of three rods glued together in the following way:

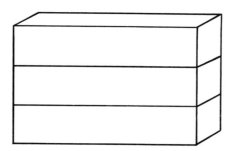

Fill in the table for the surface area of the three rods piled high, H.

Color	Length L	S	H
white	1	6	____
red	2	10	____
green	3	14	____
purple	4	18	____
yellow	5	22	46
dark green	6	26	____
black	7	30	____
brown	8	34	____
blue	9	38	____
orange	10	42	____

{ How many lengths? _____
How many ends? _____

Look for patterns in your table.

Write the formula: H = (____ × L) + ____. Explain.

Write the formula: H = (____ × S) − (____ × L). Explain.

Show that both of these formulas check the values in this table.

From Here to There with Cuisenaire Rods   © 1981 Cuisenaire Company of America, Inc.

Painting Three Rods Glued Together

Pretend that the white rod is a rubber stamp and that you are going to paint the entire surface of three rods glued together in the following way:

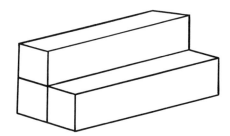

Fill in the table for the surface area of the three rods which build a bench, B.

Color	Length L	S	B	
white	1	6	____	
red	2	10	____	
green	3	14	____	
purple	4	18	____	How many lengths? _____
yellow	5	22	46	How many ends? _____
dark green	6	26	____	
black	7	30	____	
brown	8	34	____	
blue	9	38	____	
orange	10	42	____	

Look for patterns in your table.

Write the formula: B = (____ × L)+ ____. Explain.

Write the formula: B = (____ × S) – (____ × L). Explain.

Show that both of these formulas check the values in this table.

Painting More Rod Designs

Pretend that the white rod is a rubber stamp and that you are going to paint the entire surface of two rods glued together in the following way:

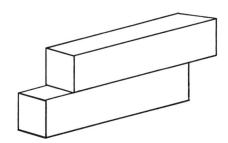

Fill in the table for the surface area of the two rods pushed over by a white rod, P.

Color	Length L	S	T	P
white	1	6	10	_12_
red	2	10	16	___
green	3	14	22	___
purple	4	18	28	___
yellow	5	22	34	_36_
dark green	6	26	40	___
black	7	30	46	___
brown	8	34	52	___
blue	9	38	58	___
orange	10	42	64	___

{ How many lengths?_____
{ How many more?_____

Look for patterns in your table.

Write the formula: P = (___ × L) + ___. Explain.

Write the formula: P = (___ × S) - [___ × (L – 1)]. Explain.

Write the formula: P = (___ × T) + ___. Explain.

Show that all of these formulas check the values in this table. Can you write any more formulas for P?

From Here to There with Cuisenaire Rods   © 1981 Cuisenaire Company of America, Inc.

Painting More Rod Designs

Pretend that the white rod is a rubber stamp and that you are going to paint the entire surface of three rods glued together in the following way:

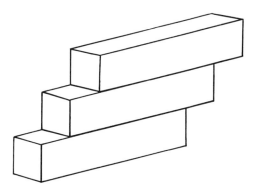

Fill in the table for the surface area of the three rods pushed over on each layer by a white rod to make the jagged design, J.

Color	Length L	S	H	P	J
white	1	6	14	12	___
red	2	10	22	18	___
green	3	14	30	24	___
purple	4	18	38	30	___
yellow	5	22	46	36	_50_
dark green	6	26	54	42	___
black	7	30	62	48	___
brown	8	34	70	54	___
blue	9	38	78	60	___
orange	10	42	86	66	___

{ How many lengths?_____
{ How many more?_____

Look for patterns in your table.

Write the formula: J = (____ × L) + ____. Explain.

Write the formula: J = (____ × S) - [____ x (L – 1)]. Explain.

Write the formula: J = (____ × H) + ____. Explain.

Write a formula that relates J and P. Show that all of the formulas check the values in this table. _____

Painting Rectangular Solids

Pretend that the white rod is a rubber stamp and that you are going to paint the entire surface of the four rods glued together in the following way.

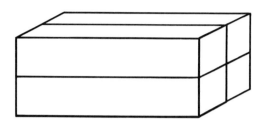

Fill in the table for the surface area of the four rod rectangular solid, F.

Color	Length L	S	T	F
white	1	6	10	_____
red	2	10	16	_____
green	3	14	22	_____
purple	4	18	28	_____
yellow	5	22	34	48
dark green	6	26	40	_____
black	7	30	46	_____
brown	8	34	52	_____
blue	9	38	58	_____
orange	10	42	64	_____

For yellow row: { How many lengths?_____ How many ends?_____

Look for patterns in your table.

Write the formula: F = (____ × L) + ____. Explain.

Write the formula: F = (____ × S) – (____ × L). Explain.

Write the formula: F = (____ × T) – (____ × L). Explain.

Show that all three formulas check the values in this table.

Can you write any more formulas for F? _____

From Here to There with Cuisenaire Rods © 1981 Cuisenaire Company of America. Inc.

Painting Square Patterns

Pretend that the white rod is a rubber stamp and that you are going to paint the entire surface of square patterns built with rods, as shown:

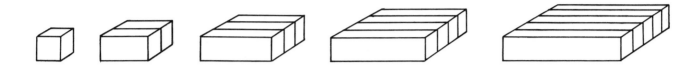

Fill in the table for the surface area of the square patterns, Q.

Color	L	Q	
white	1	____	
red	2	____	
green	3	____	
purple	4	____	How many 5 × 5 squares on
yellow	5	70	the top and bottom? _____
dark green	6	____	How many lengths on the sides? _____
black	7	____	
brown	8	____	
blue	9	____	
orange	10	____	

Look for patterns in your table.

Write the formula: Q = [____ × (L × L)] + (____ × L).

Show that the formula checks the values in this table.

Building with White Rods

Take four yellow rods and build this design.

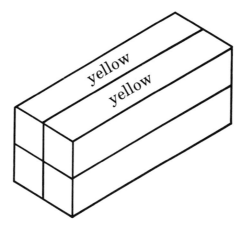

Now build this same shape with white rods.

Count how many white rods are needed. The answer is 20.

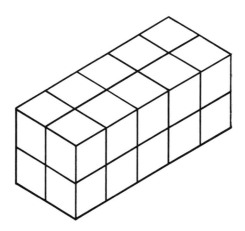

The white rods (cubes) represent the VOLUME in cubic units. The volume equals 20 cubic units.

    From Here to There with Cuisenaire Rods

Building with White Rods

Build each of these designs with the colored rods as shown. Then build each design with white rods (cubes) to find the volume of each design in cubic units.

1)

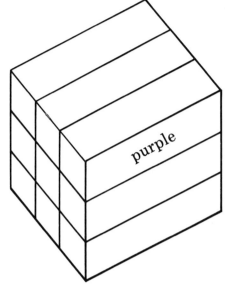

Volume: ____ cubic units

2)

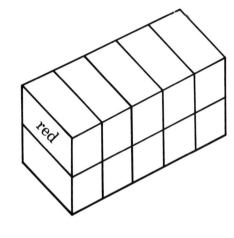

Volume: ____ cubic units

3)

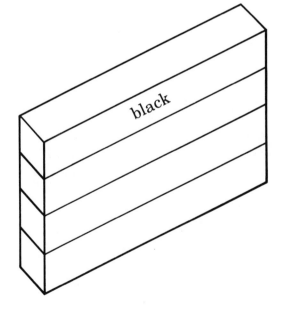

Volume: ____ cubic units

4)

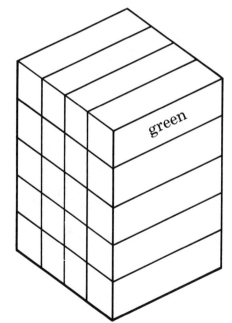

Volume: ____ cubic units

Finding the Volume of Rod Designs

Each of these designs has been built with rods as shown. What is the volume of each design in terms of cubic units (white rods)? You may wish to build the designs either with colored rods or with white rods.

1)

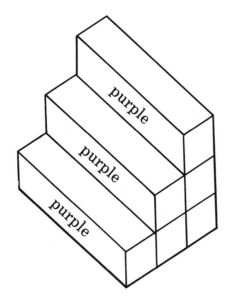

Volume: ____ cubic units

2)

Volume: ____ cubic units

3)

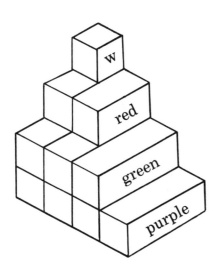

Volume: ____ cubic units

4)

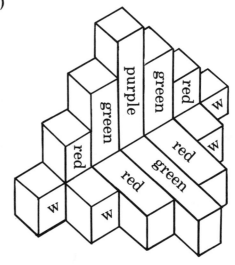

Volume: ____ cubic units

From Here to There with Cuisenaire Rods

Finding the Volume of Rod Designs

Each of these designs has been built with rods as shown. What is the volume of each design in terms of cubic units (white rods)? You may wish to build the designs either with colored rods or with white rods.

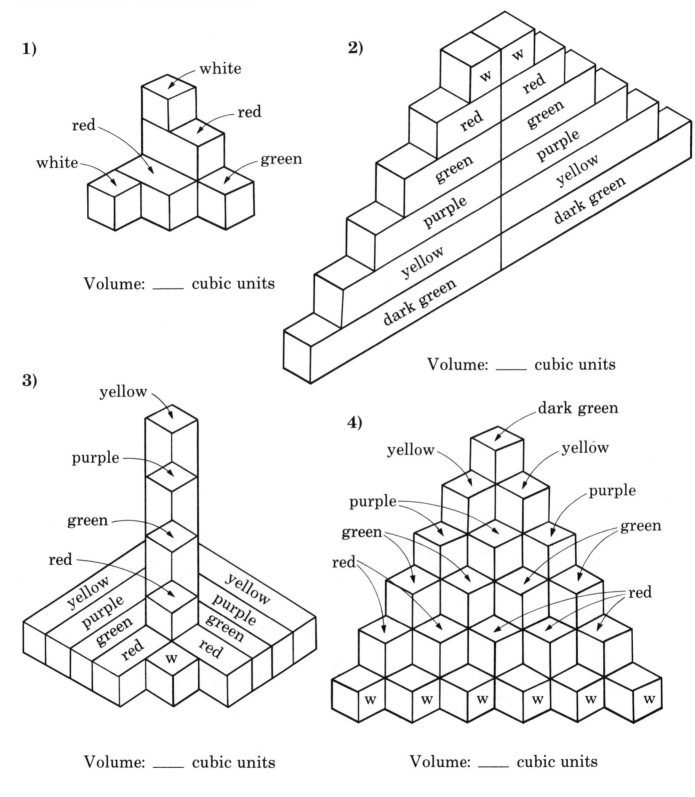

1)

Volume: ____ cubic units

2)

Volume: ____ cubic units

3)

Volume: ____ cubic units

4)

Volume: ____ cubic units

Finding the Volume of Larger Rod Designs

Each of these designs has been made with rods as shown. You may wish to build them with colored rods. What is the volume of each design in terms of cubic units (white rods)?

1)

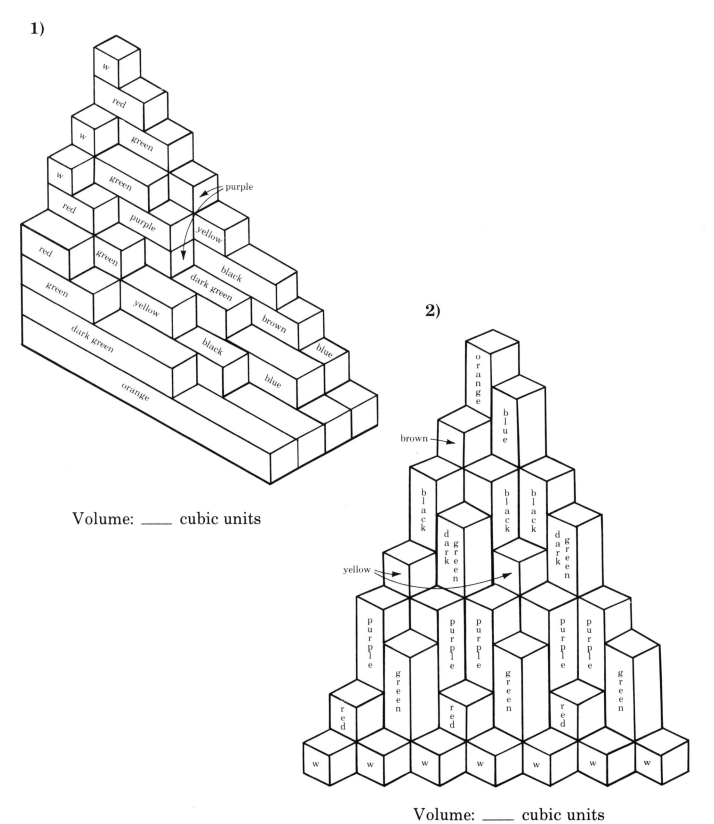

Volume: _____ cubic units

2)

Volume: _____ cubic units

From Here to There with Cuisenaire Rods   © 1981 Cuisenaire Company of America, Inc.

Finding the Volume of Larger Rod Designs

Each of these designs has been made with rods as shown. You may wish to build them with colored rods. What is the volume of each design in terms of cubic units (white rods)?

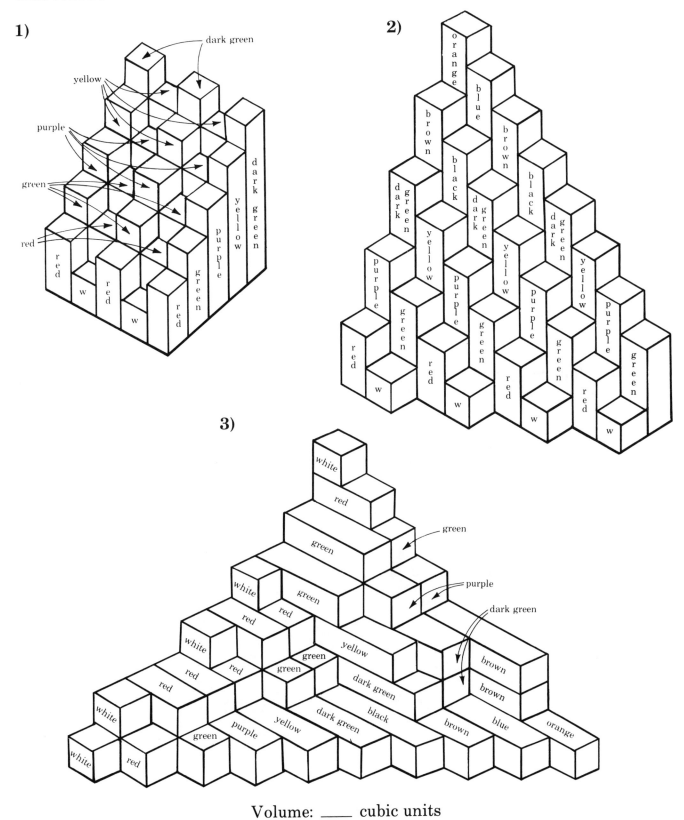

1)

2)

3)

Volume: _____ cubic units

Building Designs with White Rods

Build each of these designs with white rods. The number of white rods needed for each is given so that you can check yourself.

Caution: Hidden Rods!

1)

Volume: 15 cubic units

2)

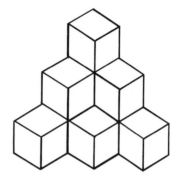

Volume: 10 cubic units

3)

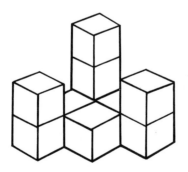

Volume: 10 cubic units

4)

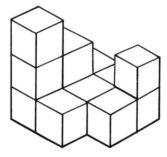

Volume: 12 cubic units

From Here to There with Cuisenaire Rods   © 1981 Cuisenaire Company of America, Inc.

Building Designs with White Rods

Build each of these designs with white rods. Count how many white rods it takes to build each design.

Caution: Hidden Rods!

1)

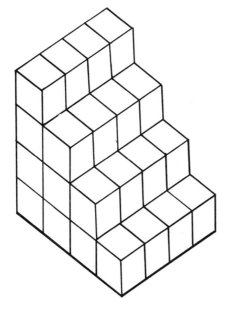

Volume: ____ cubic units

2)

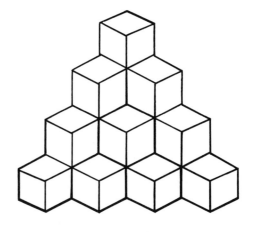

Volume: ____ cubic units

3)

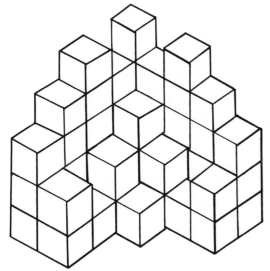

Volume: ____ cubic units

4)

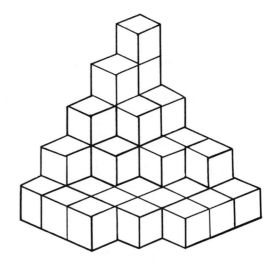

Volume: ____ cubic units

Building Larger and Larger Cubes

Build larger and larger cubes with the rods as shown:

white cube   red cube   green cube

purple cube   yellow cube

Fill in the table for the volume of each of these cubes

Color	Dimensions	Volume (cubic units)
white	1 × 1 × 1	1
red	2 × 2 × 2	8
green	____ × ____ × ____	____
purple	____ × ____ × ____	____
yellow	____ × ____ × ____	____

From Here to There with Cuisenaire Rods   © 1981 Cuisenaire Company of America, Inc.

Comparing Surface Area and Volume of Cubes

Pretend to build a cube for each color of rods (white cube, red cube, green cube, ... orange cube).

Then pretend to paint the outside surface of each cube to find the surface area in square units.

Then pretend to build each colored cube with white cubes to find the volume in cubic units.

Then find the ratio: $\dfrac{\text{Surface Area}}{\text{Volume}}$

Complete the table below:

Color	Dimensions	Surface Area (square units)	Volume (cubic units)	Ratio of Surface Area / Volume
white	1 × 1 × 1	6	1	$\frac{6}{1}$
red	2 × 2 × 2	24	8	$\frac{24}{8} = \frac{3}{1}$
green	3 × 3 × 3	54	27	$\frac{54}{27} = \frac{2}{1}$
purple	__×__×__	___	___	___
yellow	__×__×__	___	___	___
dark green	__×__×__	___	___	___
black	__×__×__	___	___	___
brown	__×__×__	___	___	___
blue	__×__×__	___	___	___
orange	__×__×__	___	___	___

This problem helps to explain why only large animals live in cold climates and why your fingers and nose get extremely cold in cold weather. Can you explain why?

Selected Answers and Comments

Pages 1-16: General Comments

The concept of area with rods is viewed as the number of square units enclosed within the "footprint" which the rod makes on centimeter graph paper. Note that it is not correct to talk about the area of a rod, because each rod has six surface areas, four sides and two ends. Surface area is treated starting on page 31.

Page 2: 1) 5 2) 7 3) 8 4) 10

Page 3: The challenge of finding the specified number of rods to make each design can be treated as a spatial problem solving task. For example in 2), there are many ways to use eight rods, two of which are shown; while in 3), there is only one way.

2) Two possible ways:

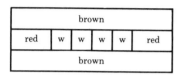

3) Only one possible way:

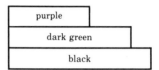

Some students may enjoy finding all possible ways. Work of this nature gives students the versatility with the rods which will be necessary in more difficult problem solving tasks such as on pages 29 and 30.

Answers for the Areas: 1) 10   2) 24   3) 17   4) 40   **Page 4:** 1) 24 2) 26 3) 28 4) 50

Page 5:

1)
$$\begin{array}{r} 15 \\ 12 \\ \hline 27 \end{array}$$

2)
$$\begin{array}{r} 15 \\ 12 \\ \hline 27 \end{array}$$

3)
$$\begin{array}{r} 3 \times 7 = 21 \\ 3 \times 2 = 6 \\ \hline 27 \end{array}$$

4) There are many different ways. Students may need to provide more multiplication problems. No matter how it is done, the area will be 27 square units.

Page 6:

1)
$$\begin{array}{r} 15 \\ 9 \\ 14 \\ \hline 38 \end{array}$$

2)
$$\begin{array}{r} 3 \times 8 = 24 \\ 3 \times 2 = 6 \\ 2 \times 4 = 8 \\ \hline 38 \end{array}$$

3) and 4) There are many different ways. Students may need to provide more multiplication problems. No matter how it is done, the area will be 38 square units.

Page 7:

1)
$$\begin{array}{r} 36 \\ 28 \\ 4 \times 5 = 20 \\ 4 \times 3 = 12 \\ 4 \times 1 = 4 \\ \hline 100 \end{array}$$

2) There are many different ways, the simplest:

$$10 \times 10 = 100.$$

Page 8:

1)
$$\begin{array}{r} 40 \\ 32 \\ 4 \times 6 = 24 \\ 4 \times 4 = 16 \\ 4 \times 2 = 8 \\ 1 \times 1 = 1 \\ \hline 121 \end{array}$$

2) There are many different ways, the simplest:

$$11 \times 11 = 121.$$

Page 9: Students should be encouraged to compute the area in various ways; such as adding all of the individual areas, counting rods of the same color and using multiplication combinations, or taking all the rods and building some other design that might simplify the computation (such as the grouping by tens shown below).

One possible arrangement for simplifying the problem:

The rods will build a 10 x 10 square with one white rod short.

99 square units

red	red	red	red	w	w
green	green	green	red		
green	green	green			
purple	purple	**red**			
purple	purple	**red**			
purple	purple	**red**			
dark green	purple				
dark green	purple				
yellow	yellow				
purple	purple	w			

w

Student should check to see that they get the same area regardless of the method used:

Page 10:   1) 52   2) 58

Pages 11-14: The same area is obtained no matter how the designs are covered with rods. Students may wish to record the color names to show how they chose to place the rods on each design. Pages 13 and 14 offer problem solving challenges as well as practice in finding area.

Page 11:   Area: 1) 28   2) 34   3) 49   4) 34
            Minimum number of rods: 1) 6   2) 6   3) 9   4) 5
Page 12:   Area: 1) 25   2) 30   3) 41   4) 28
            Minimum number of rods: 1) 5   2) 5   3) 9   4) 6
Page 13:   Area: 1) 36   2) 34   3) 34   4) 31
            Minimum number of rods: 1) 8   2) 7   3) 6   4) 7
Page 14:   Area: 1) 44   2) 30   3) 44   4) 30
            Minimum number of rods: 1) 8   2) 5   3) 9   4) 7

Page 15: These puzzles involve finding the fewest number of rods that can be used and the greatest number of rods that can be used to cover a region. The greatest number always follows the same pattern: cover with all white rods; the number of white rods used is the same number as the number of units of area. The fewest number of rods that can be used offers a challenge, as rods can be placed both horizontally and vertically on the same design. Students will need to explore many ways of maneuvering the rods and will need to compare their answers and strategies. There is no simple solution to finding the fewest number of rods for any design.

Area: 1) 38   2) 38   3) 58   Fewest number of rods: 1) 7   2) 7   3) 9

Greatest number of rods: 1) 38   2) 38   3) 58

Page 16: This page adds the further challenge of finding the number of sides of the figure. Once students have solved these problems, they should be encouraged to make some area problems of their own to be shared and solved by their classmates.   1) 6

2) One possible figure:

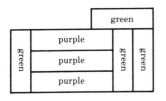

3) One possible figure:

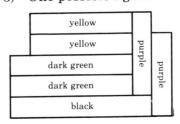

4) One possible figure:

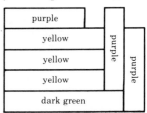

Pages 17-24: General Comments

The concept of perimeter with rods is viewed as the number of units of length in the outline of the tracing of a rod or rod design. It is important for students to realize that the perimeter of a rod is not the same as its "length." For example, the perimeter of the outline of a dark green rod is 14 units; whereby the "length" of a dark green rod is 6.

Page 18:   1) 12   2) 10   3) 16   4) 18
Page 19:   1) 14   2) 18   3) 20   **Page 20:**   1) 30   2) 28   3) 26   4) 36
Page 21:   1) 16   2) 18   3) 26   4) 26   5) 18   6) 22

At this point in the development of perimeter, it is interesting to note an important difference between perimeter and area. When the same three rods, such as green, purple and yellow, are used to make various designs, many different perimeters are possible; yet only one value of area is possible. The perimeters range from a minimum of 16 units of length to a maximum of 26 units. As shown in 3) and 4), it is possible to have more than one design with the same perimeter. The problems given have answers 16, 18, 22 and 26. The other even values of 20 and 24 are also possible perimeters. Students might enjoy creating designs with these values for perimeter and recording them on a sheet of graph paper.

Page 22:　　1) 18　　2) 28　　　　　Three possible designs with different perimeters:

3) 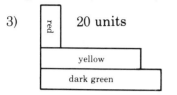 20 units

4)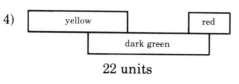

22 units

5)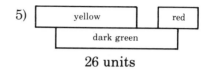

26 units

Using a red, yellow and dark green rod, students should be able to make designs with perimeters 18, 20, 22, 24, 26 and 28. Some students may wish to find more than one design for each perimeter.

Page 23:　　One possible design for each:

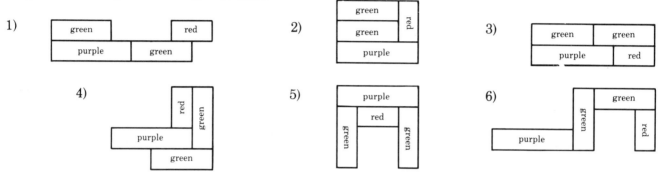

The smallest possible perimeter is 14 and the largest is 26. All of the even values are possible between 14 and 26. Some students may notice that the perimeter of a rod design traced on graph paper always results in an even number for the perimeter. However if rods were placed in half-way positions,

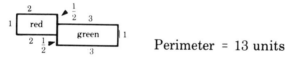 Perimeter = 13 units

the perimeter could be odd. This possibility raises all kinds of new explorations for those students capable of handling fractional parts and more difficult spatial reasoning.

Page 24:　　One possible design for each:

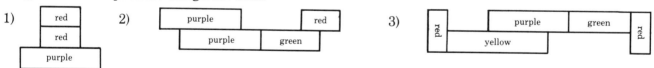

Once students have solved these problems, they should be encouraged to make some perimeter problems of their own to be shared and solved by their classmates.

Pages 25-30: General Comments

In the previous separate sections on area and perimeter, students may have observed some of the interrelationships between the two concepts. For example, given the same rods to build various designs, the area remains constant while various perimeters are possible. The smaller perimeter values arise when the rod design is more "compact" (the tracing approaching the shape of a square), and the larger perimeter values occur when the rod design is less "compact" (approaching being strung out in a linear fashion). For example, see the answers for page 23, exercise 2 and 6.

　　　From Here to There with Cuisenaire Rods　　© 1981 Cuisenaire Company of America, Inc.

Pages 25, 26: These two pages explore the various rectangular rod designs that can be made with a constant value for the area. In each case, the various values for the perimeter lead to the conclusion that the minimum perimeter occurs when the rectangle is a square.

Pages 25:

Width	Length	Area	Perimeter	
4	9	36	26	
1	36	36	74	
2	18	36	40	
3	12	36	30	
6	6	36	24	Minimum perimeter,
9	4	36	26	6 × 6 square
12	3	36	30	
18	2	36	40	
36	1	36	74	

Page 26:

1)
Width	Length	Area	Perimeter	
1	16	16	34	
2	8	16	20	Minimum perimeter,
4	4	16	16	4 × 4 square
8	2	16	20	
16	1	16	34	

2)
Width	Length	Area	Perimeter	
1	25	25	52	Minimum perimeter,
5	5	25	20	5 x 5 square
25	1	25	52	

3)
Width	Length	Area	Perimeter	
1	64	64	130	
2	32	64	68	
4	16	64	40	Minimum perimeter,
8	8	64	32	8 × 8 square
16	4	64	40	
32	2	64	68	
64	1	64	130	

4)
Width	Length	Area	Perimeter	
1	100	100	202	
2	50	100	104	
4	25	100	58	
5	20	100	50	Minimum perimeter,
10	10	100	40	10 × 10 square
20	5	100	50	
25	4	100	58	
50	2	100	104	
100	1	100	202	

Pages 27, 28: These two pages explore the various rectangular rod designs that can be made with a constant value for the perimeter. In each case, the maximum area occurs when the rectangle is a square.

Page 27:

Width	Length	Perimeter	Area	
1	11	24	11	
2	10	24	20	
3	9	24	27	
4	8	24	32	
5	7	24	35	
6	6	24	36	Maximum area,
7	5	24	35	6 × 6 square
8	4	24	32	
9	3	24	27	
10	2	24	20	
11	1	24	11	

Page 28:

1)
Width	Length	Perimeter	Area	
1	5	12	5	
2	4	12	8	Maximum area,
3	3	12	9	3 × 3 square
4	2	12	8	
5	1	12	5	

2)
Width	Length	Perimeter	Area	
1	9	20	9	
2	8	20	16	
3	7	20	21	
4	6	20	24	Maximum area,
5	5	20	25	5 × 5 square
6	4	20	24	
7	3	20	21	
8	2	20	16	
9	1	20	9	

3) Width	Length	Perimeter	Area	
1	13	28	13	
2	12	28	24	
3	11	28	33	
4	10	28	40	
5	9	28	45	
6	8	28	48	
7	7	28	49	Maximum area, 7 × 7 square
8	6	28	48	
9	5	28	45	
10	4	28	40	
11	3	28	33	
12	2	28	24	
13	1	28	13	

4) Width	Length	Perimeter	Area	
1	15	32	15	
2	14	32	28	
3	13	32	39	
4	12	32	48	
5	11	32	55	
6	10	32	60	
7	9	32	63	
8	8	32	64	Maximum area, 8 × 8 square
9	7	32	63	
10	6	32	60	
11	5	32	55	
12	4	32	48	
13	3	32	39	
14	2	32	28	
15	1	32	15	

Students may wish to explore the more general problem of maximizing the area for a given perimeter to find that the circle is the optimal figure. This problem has practical considerations when one needs to build a fence or a play pen for animals.

Pages 29, 30: These problems may be very challenging and motivating for your students, especially those on page 30 where the students first have to select the rods. Each problem has many right answers, as many different rod configurations fulfill the required conditions. One possible solution is shown for each problem.

Page 29: One possible solution for each:

Page 30: One possible solution for each:

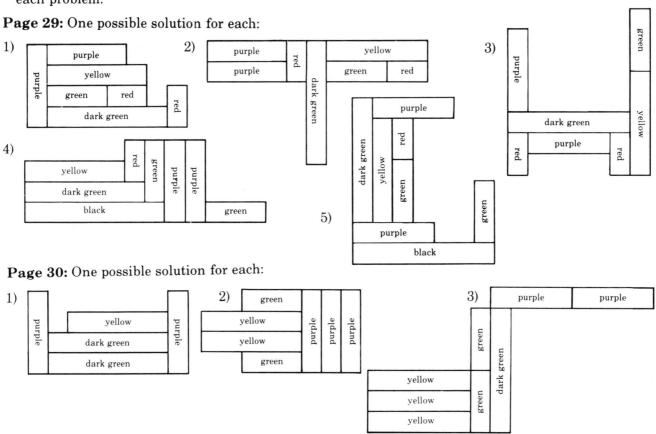

From Here to There with Cuisenaire Rods   © 1981 Cuisenaire Company of America, Inc.

The concept of surface area with rods is the number of square units on the entire outer surface of a rod or rod design. A motivating way for students to view the surface area of a rod design is to pretend that the white rod is a rubber stamp and to find the fewest number of times needed to "paint" the surface of the rod design. Patterns leading to generalized formulas emerge when rod designs are explored for the whole spectrum of rod colors.

Page 31:   6   26   26 square units

Page 32:

L	Surface Area S	Verification of values: $S = (4 \times L) + 2$
1	6	$S = (4 \times 1) + 2 = 6$
2	10	$S = (4 \times 2) + 2 = 10$
3	14	$S = (4 \times 3) + 2 = 14$
4	18	$S = (4 \times 4) + 2 = 18$
5	22	$S = (4 \times 5) + 2 = 22$
6	26	$S = (4 \times 6) + 2 = 26$
7	30	$S = (4 \times 7) + 2 = 30$
8	34	$S = (4 \times 8) + 2 = 34$
9	38	$S = (4 \times 9) + 2 = 38$
10	42	$S = (4 \times 10) + 2 = 42$

As the rod lengths increase consecutively, the surface area increases by 4, as there is one extra unit of area on each of the four rod lengths. The two ends of the rod are indicated by the +2 in the formula.

Page 33: Students can view this problem in more than one way. Checking the values in each formula:

L	S	T	$T = (6 \times L) + 4$	$T = (2 \times S) - (2 \times L)$
1	6	10	$T = (6 \times 1) + 4 = 10$	$T = (2 \times 6) - (2 \times 1) = 10$
2	10	16	$T = (6 \times 2) + 4 = 16$	$T = (2 \times 10) - (2 \times 2) = 16$
3	14	22	$T = (6 \times 3) + 4 = 22$	$T = (2 \times 14) - (2 \times 3) = 22$
4	18	28	$T = (6 \times 4) + 4 = 28$	$T = (2 \times 18) - (2 \times 4) = 28$
5	22	34	$T = (6 \times 5) + 4 = 34$	$T = (2 \times 22) - (2 \times 5) = 34$
6	26	40	$T = (6 \times 6) + 4 = 40$	$T = (2 \times 26) - (2 \times 6) = 40$
7	30	46	$T = (6 \times 7) + 4 = 46$	$T = (2 \times 30) - (2 \times 7) = 46$
8	34	52	$T = (6 \times 8) + 4 = 52$	$T = (2 \times 34) - (2 \times 8) = 52$
9	38	58	$T = (6 \times 9) + 4 = 58$	$T = (2 \times 38) - (2 \times 9) = 58$
10	42	64	$T = (6 \times 10) + 4 = 64$	$T = (2 \times 42) - (2 \times 10) = 64$

The formula $T = (6 \times L) + 4$ comes from viewing the surface area as being made up of 6 rod lengths plus the 4 ends.
The formula $T = (2 \times S) - (2 \times L)$ comes from viewing the surface area as twice the surface area of separate rods minus the two lengths which are glued together and hence do not get "painted."

Page 34: Students can view this problem in more than one way. Checking the values in each formula:

L	S	E	E = (8 × L) + 2	E = (2 × S) − 2
1	6	10	E = (8 × 1) + 2 = 10	E = (2 × 6) − 2 = 10
2	10	18	E = (8 × 2) + 2 = 18	E = (2 × 10) − 2 = 18
3	14	26	E = (8 × 3) + 2 = 26	E = (2 × 14) − 2 = 26
4	18	34	E = (8 × 4) + 2 = 34	E = (2 × 18) − 2 = 34
5	22	42	E = (8 × 5) + 2 = 42	E = (2 × 22) − 2 = 42
6	26	50	E = (8 × 6) + 2 = 50	E = (2 × 26) − 2 = 50
7	30	58	E = (8 × 7) + 2 = 58	E = (2 × 30) − 2 = 58
8	34	66	E = (8 × 8) + 2 = 66	E = (2 × 34) − 2 = 66
9	38	74	E = (8 × 9) + 2 = 74	E = (2 × 38) − 2 = 74
10	42	82	E = (8 × 10 + 2 = 82	E = (2 × 42) − 2 = 82

The formula E = (8 × L) + 2 comes from viewing the surface area as being made up of 8 rod lengths plus the 2 ends.

The formula E = (2 × S) − 2 comes from viewing the surface area as twice the surface area of separate rods minus the two ends which are glued together and hence don't get painted.

Page 35: Students can view this problem in more than one way. Checking the values in each formula:

L	S	H	H = (8 × L) + 6	H = (3 × S) − (4 × L)
1	6	14	H = (8 × 1) + 6 = 14	H = (3 × 6) − (4 × 1) = 14
2	10	22	H = (8 × 2) + 6 = 22	H = (3 × 10) − (4 × 2) = 22
3	14	30	H = (8 × 3) + 6 = 30	H = (3 × 14) − (4 × 3) = 30
4	18	38	H = (8 × 4) + 6 = 38	H = (3 × 18) − (4 × 4) = 38
5	22	46	H = (8 × 5) + 6 = 46	H = (3 × 22) − (4 × 5) = 46
6	26	54	H = (8 × 6) + 6 = 54	H = (3 × 26) − (4 × 6) = 54
7	30	62	H = (8 × 7) + 6 = 62	H = (3 × 30) − (4 × 7) = 62
8	34	70	H = (8 × 8) + 6 = 70	H = (3 × 34) − (4 × 8) = 70
9	38	78	H = (8 × 9) + 6 = 78	H = (3 × 38) − (4 × 9) = 78
10	42	86	H = (8 × 10) + 6 = 86	H = (3 × 42) − (4 × 10) = 86

The formula H = (8 × L) + 6 comes from viewing the surface area as being made up of 8 rod lengths plus the 6 ends.

The formula H = (3 × S) − (4 × L) comes from viewing the surface area as three times the surface area of separate rods minus the four lengths which are hidden inside because of the gluing.

Page 36: Students can view this problem in more than one way. Some may be surprised initially that these answers are the same as the ones for the problem on page 35. Checking the values in each formula:

L	S	B	B = (8 × L) + 6	B = (3 × S) − (4 × L)
1	6	14	B = (8 × 1) + 6 = 14	B = (3 × 6) − (4 × 1) = 14
2	10	22	B = (8 × 2) + 6 = 22	B = (3 × 10) − (4 × 2) = 22
3	14	30	B = (8 × 3) + 6 = 30	B = (3 × 14) − (4 × 3) = 30
4	18	38	B = (8 × 4) + 6 = 38	B = (3 × 18) − (4 × 4) = 38
5	22	46	B = (8 × 5) + 6 = 46	B = (3 × 22) − (4 × 5) = 46
6	26	54	B = (8 × 6) + 6 = 54	B = (3 × 26) − (4 × 6) = 54
7	30	62	B = (8 × 7) + 6 = 62	B = (3 × 30) − (4 × 7) = 62
8	34	70	B = (8 × 8) + 6 = 70	B = (3 × 34) − (4 × 8) = 70
9	38	78	B = (8 × 9) + 6 = 78	B = (3 × 38) − (4 × 9) = 78
10	42	86	B = (8 × 10) + 6 = 86	B = (3 × 42) − (4 × 10) = 86

This formula B = (8 × L) + 6 comes from viewing the surface area as being made up of 8 rod lengths plus the 6 ends.

The formula B = (3 × S) − (4 x L) comes from viewing the surface area as three times the surface area of separate rods minus the four lengths which are hidden inside because of the gluing.

From Here to There with Cuisenaire Rods

Page 37: Students can view this problem in several ways. Some may be surprised initially that these answers are not the same as the ones for the problem on page 33. Checking the values in each formula:

L	S	T	P	P = (6 × L) + 6	P = (2 × S) - [2 × (L - 1)]	P = (1 × T) + 2
1	6	10	12	P = (6 × 1) + 6 = 12	P = (2 × 6) - [2 × (1 - 1)] = 12	P = (1 × 10) + 2 = 12
2	10	16	18	P = (6 × 2) + 6 = 18	P = (2 × 10) - [2 × (2 - 1)] = 18	P = (1 × 16) + 2 = 18
3	14	22	24	P = (6 × 3) + 6 = 24	P = (2 × 14) - [2 × (3 - 1)] = 24	P = (1 × 22) + 2 = 24
4	18	28	30	P = (6 × 4) + 6 = 30	P = (2 × 18) - [2 × (4 - 1)] = 30	P = (1 × 28) + 2 = 30
5	22	34	36	P = (6 × 5) + 6 = 36	P = (2 × 22) - [2 × (5 - 1)] = 36	P = (1 × 34) + 2 = 36
6	26	40	42	P = (6 × 6) + 6 = 42	P = (2 × 26) - [2 × (6 - 1)] = 42	P = (1 × 40) + 2 = 42
7	30	46	48	P = (6 × 7) + 6 = 48	P = (2 × 30) - [2 × (7 - 1)] = 48	P = (1 × 46) + 2 = 48
8	34	52	54	P = (6 × 8) + 6 = 54	P = (2 × 34) - [2 × (8 - 1)] = 54	P = (1 × 52) + 2 = 54
9	38	58	60	P = (6 × 9) + 6 = 60	P = (2 × 38) - [2 × (9 - 1)] = 60	P = (1 × 58) + 2 = 60
10	42	64	66	P = (6 × 10) + 6 = 66	P = (2 × 42) - [2 × (10 - 1)] = 66	P = (1 × 64) + 2 = 66

The formula P = (6 × L) + 6 comes from viewing the surface area as being made up of 6 rod lengths plus 6 square units of area at the ends.

The formula P = (2 × S) - [2 x (L - 1)] comes from viewing the surface area as twice the surface area of separate rods minus the two hidden sections which are each one square unit less than the rod length.

The formula P = (1 × T) + 2 comes from viewing this configuration as just 2 square units more than the surface area of two rods glued together and not pushed over.

Another formula for P might be: P = (8 × L)   - 2 × (L - 1)   + 4

8 lengths in all, minus the hidden part, plus the 4 ends

Page 38: Students can view this problem in several ways. Checking the values in each formula:

L	S	H	P	J	J = (8 × L) + 10	J = (3 × S) - [4 × (L - 1)]	J = (1 × H) + 4
1	6	14	12	18	J = (8 × 1) + 10 = 18	J = (3 × 6) - [4 × (1 - 1)] = 18	J = (1 × 14) + 4 = 18
2	10	22	18	26	J = (8 × 2) + 10 = 26	J = (3 × 10) - [4 × (2 - 1)] = 26	J = (1 × 22) + 4 = 26
3	14	30	24	34	J = (8 × 3) + 10 = 34	J = (3 × 14) - [4 × (3 - 1)] = 34	J = (1 × 30) + 4 = 34
4	18	38	30	42	J = (8 × 4) + 10 = 42	J = (3 × 18) - [4 × (4 - 1)] = 42	J = (1 × 38) + 4 = 42
5	22	46	36	50	J = (8 × 5) + 10 = 50	J = (3 × 22) - [4 × (5 - 1)] = 50	J = (1 × 46) + 4 = 50
6	26	54	42	58	J = (8 × 6) + 10 = 58	J = (3 × 26) - [4 × (6 - 1)] = 58	J = (1 × 54) + 4 = 58
7	30	62	48	66	J = (8 × 7) + 10 = 66	J = (3 × 30) - [4 × (7 - 1)] = 66	J = (1 × 62) + 4 = 66
8	34	70	54	74	J = (8 × 8) + 10 = 74	J = (3 × 34) - [4 × (8 - 1)] = 74	J = (1 × 70) + 4 = 74
9	38	78	60	82	J = (8 × 9) + 10 = 82	J = (3 × 38) - [4 × (9 - 1)] = 82	J = (1 × 78) + 4 = 82
10	42	86	66	90	J = (8 × 10) + 10 = 90	J = (3 × 42) - [4 × (10 - 1)] = 90	J = (1 × 86) + 4 = 90

The formula J = (8 × L) + 10 comes from viewing the surface area as being made up of 8 rod lengths plus 10 square units of area at the ends.

The formula J = (3 x S) - [4 × (L - 1)] comes from viewing the surface area as three times the surface area of separate rods minus the 4 hidden sections which are each one square unit less than the rod length.

The formula J = (1 × H) + 4 comes from viewing this configuration as just 4 square units more than the surface area of three rods glued together and not pushed over.

Another formula for J might be: J =   (12 × L)   - 4 ×(L - 1)   + 6

12 lengths in all, minus the hidden part, plus 6 ends

Page 39: Students can view this problem in several ways. Checking the values in each formula:

L	S	T	F	F = (8 × L) + 8	F = (4 × S) − (8 × L)	F = (2 × T) − (4 × L)
1	6	10	16	F = (8 × 1) + 8 = 16	F = (4 × 6) − (8 × 1) = 16	F = (2 × 10) − (4 × 1) = 16
2	10	16	24	F = (8 × 2) + 8 = 24	F = (4 × 10) − (8 × 2) = 24	F = (2 × 16) − (4 × 2) = 24
3	14	22	32	F = (8 × 3) + 8 = 32	F = (4 × 14) − (8 × 3) = 32	F = (2 × 22) − (4 × 3) = 32
4	18	28	40	F = (8 × 4) + 8 = 40	F = (4 × 18) − (8 × 4) = 40	F = (2 × 28) − (4 × 4) = 40
5	22	34	48	F = (8 × 5) + 8 = 48	F = (4 × 22) − (8 × 5) = 48	F = (2 × 34) − (4 × 5) = 48
6	26	40	56	F = (8 × 6) + 8 = 56	F = (4 × 26) − (8 × 6) = 56	F = (2 × 40) − (4 × 6) = 56
7	30	46	64	F = (8 × 7) + 8 = 64	F = (4 × 30) − (8 × 7) = 64	F = (2 × 46) − (4 × 7) = 64
8	34	52	72	F = (8 × 8) + 8 = 72	F = (4 × 34) − (8 × 8) = 72	F = (2 × 52) − (4 × 8) = 72
9	38	58	80	F = (8 × 9) + 8 = 80	F = (4 × 38) − (8 × 9) = 80	F = (2 × 58) − (4 × 9) = 82
10	42	64	88	F = (8 × 10) + 8 = 88	F = (4 × 42) − (8 × 10 = 88	F = (2 × 64) − (4 × 10) = 88

The formula F = (8 × L + 8) comes from viewing the surface area as being made up of 8 rod lengths plus ends.

The formula F = (4 × S) − (8 × L) comes from viewing the surface area as 4 times the surface area of separate rods minus the 8 lengths which are hidden inside because of the gluing.

The formula F = (2 × T) − (4 × L) comes from viewing this surface area as 2 sets of two rods glued together. There are 4 lengths hidden inside that are not accounted for in the 2 × T.

Students may also see the surface area of a rectangular solid in terms of top, bottom, sides, and ends. They should make other rectangular solids with the rods and explore the various ways of viewing the surface area.

Page 40: Checking the values:

L	Q	Q = [2 × (L × L)] + (4 × L)
1	6	Q = [2 x (1 × 1)] + (4 × 1) = 6
2	16	Q = [2 x (2 × 2)] + (4 × 2) = 16
3	30	Q = [2 x (3 × 3)] + (4 × 3) = 30
4	48	Q = [2 x (4 × 4)] + (4 × 4) = 48
5	70	Q = [2 x (5 × 5)] + (4 × 5) = 70
6	96	Q = [2 x (6 × 6)] + (4 × 6) = 96
7	126	Q = [2 x (7 × 7)] + (4 × 7) = 126
8	160	Q = [2 x (8 × 8)] + (4 × 8) = 160
9	198	Q = [2 x (9 × 9)] + (4 × 9) = 198
10	240	Q = [2 x (10 × 10)] + (4 × 10) = 240

Pages 41-50: General Comments
The concept of volume with rods is viewed as the number of cubic units (white rods) it would take to build a rod design. Students may wish to build the designs with white rods and count the number used, or they may build the designs with colored rods and compute the volume by adding up the separate volume of each rod used. Multiplication techniques further shorten the work when more than one rod of the same color is used. These activities help students develop their spatial abilities of transforming a two-dimensional picture into a three-dimensional design. Students enjoy using the three-dimensional aspects of the rods and will want to make their own designs—both volume and surface area should be found and compared.

Page 42: 1) 36 (9 × 4)   2) 20 (10 × 2)   **Page 43:** 1) 24   2) 20   3) 30   4) 25
3) 28 (4 × 7)   4) 60 (20 × 3)

Page 44: 1) 9   2) 42   3) 43   4) 56   **Page 45:** 1) 135   2) 112

From Here to There with Cuisenaire Rods

Page 46: 1) 90   2) 122   3) 133   **Page 48:** 1) 40   2) 20   3) 51   4) 40

Page 49:

Color	Dimensions	Volume
white	1 × 1 × 1	1
red	2 × 2 × 2	8
green	3 × 3 × 3	27
purple	4 × 4 × 4	64
yellow	5 × 5 × 5	125

Page 50:

Color	Dimensions	Surface Area	Volume	Ratio of Surface Area Volume	
white	1 × 1 × 1	6	1	$\frac{6}{1}$	
red	2 × 2 × 2	24	8	$\frac{24}{8} = \frac{3}{1}$	
green	3 × 3 × 3	54	27	$\frac{54}{27} = \frac{2}{1}$	
purple	4 × 4 × 4	96	64	$\frac{96}{64} = \frac{3}{2}$	The ratios
yellow	5 × 5 × 5	150	125	$\frac{150}{125} = \frac{6}{5}$	get smaller
dark green	6 × 6 × 6	216	216	$\frac{216}{216} = 1$	as the cubes
black	7 × 7 × 7	294	343	$\frac{294}{343} = \frac{6}{7}$	get larger.
brown	8 × 8 × 8	384	512	$\frac{384}{512} = \frac{3}{4}$	
blue	9 × 9 × 9	486	729	$\frac{486}{729} = \frac{2}{3}$	
orange	10 × 10 × 10	600	1000	$\frac{600}{1000} = \frac{3}{5}$	

When the ratio of the surface area to volume is small (as with large animals) there is less heat loss than when the ratio of the surface area to volume is large (as with parts of the body like fingers and nose.)

CENTIMETER GRAPH PAPER

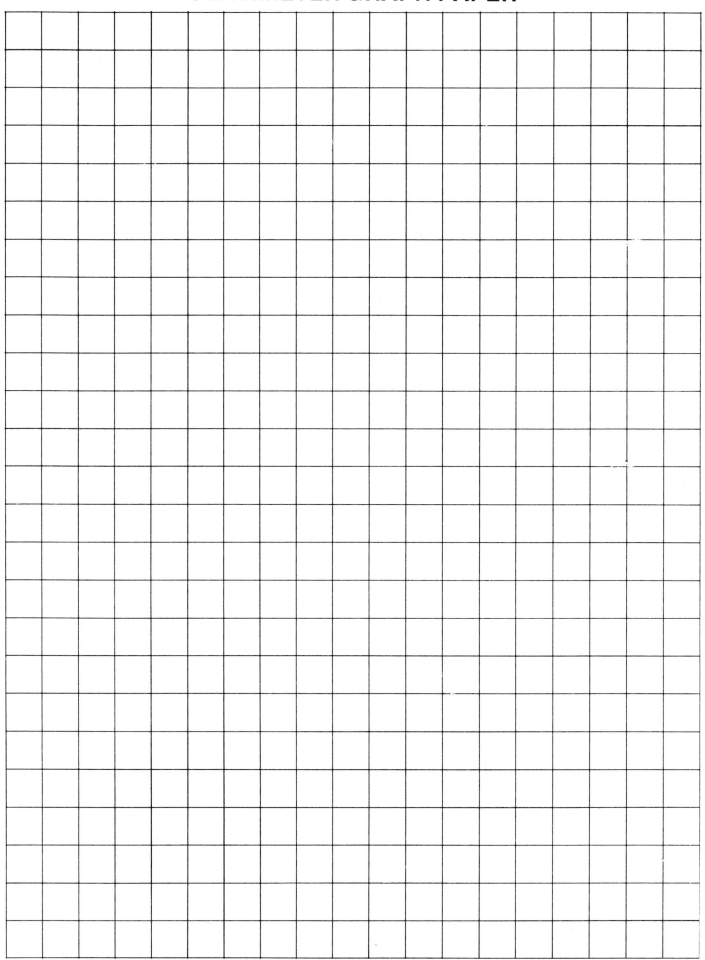